ASTOR PIAZZOLLA
for Violin & Guitar

ARRANGEMENTS BY IAN MURPHY

CONTENTS

ISBN 978-0-634-09639-6

Publisher: LES EDITIONS UNIVERSELLES
represented in Canada and USA by
DAVID MURPHY ET CIE

HAL•LEONARD® CORPORATION
7777 W. BLUEMOUND RD. P.O. BOX 13819 MILWAUKEE, WI 53213

Visit Hal Leonard Online at
www.halleonard.com

ADIOS NONINO

By YVES PAUL MARTIAL PUECH
and ASTOR PIAZZOLLA

Tempo 1 -Deciso

BORICUA

By ASTOR PIAZZOLLA

BUENOS AIRES HORA CERO

By ASTOR PIAZZOLLA

CALAMBRE

By ASTOR PIAZZOLLA

To Coda ⊕   D.S. al Coda   ⊕ CODA

DECARISIMO

By ASTOR PIAZZOLLA

DERNIER LAMENTO

By ROGER AUGUSTE, CHARLES DESBOIS,
ALBERT ABRAHAM, BEN SOUSSAN
and ASTOR PIAZZOLLA

To Coda ⊕

D.S. al Coda

CODA
⊕

DÉTRESSE

By ASTOR PIAZZOLLA

EXTASIS

By ASTOR PIAZZOLLA

FIÈVRE
(Fiebre de tango)

By ALBERT ABRAHAM, BEN SOUSSAN
and ALBERT NOEL DE MARIGNY ENGEURRAND

Violin

Guitar
Capo I

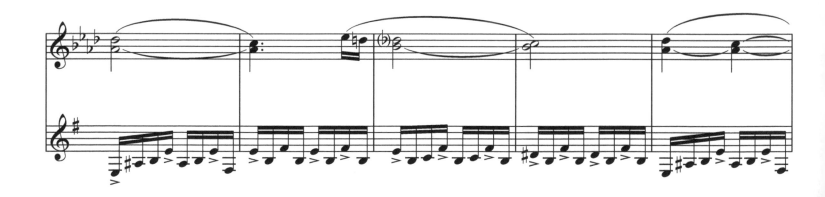

FRACANAPA

By ASTOR PIAZZOLLA

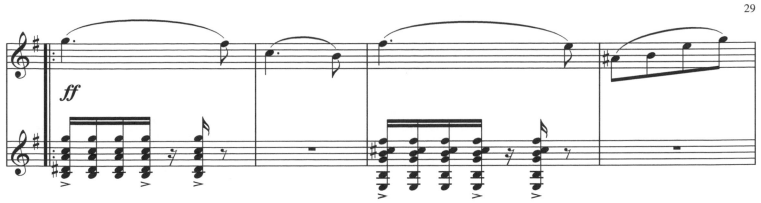

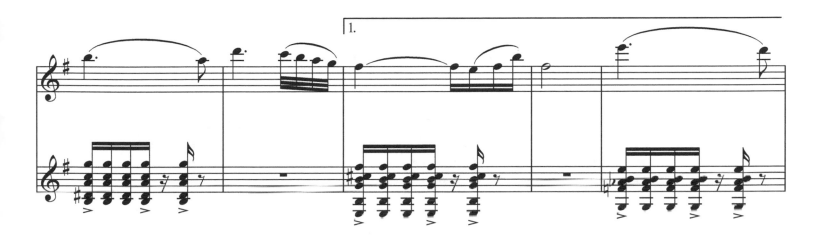

D.C. al Fine

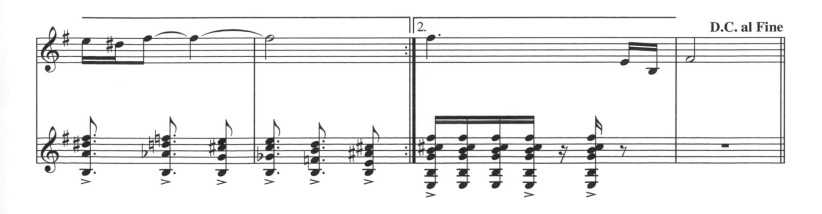

GREENWICH

By ALBERT ABRAHAM, BEN SOUSSAN,
ANDRE PSIETO and ASTOR PIAZZOLLA

GULINAY

By ASTOR PIAZZOLLA

IMÁGINES 676

By ASTOR PIAZZOLLA

IRACUNDO

By ASTOR PIAZZOLLA

Lento

(Key change is for repeat only)   **Fine**

LA CALLE 92

By ASTOR PIAZZOLLA

D.C. al Fine

LA FIN DEL MUNDO

By OSCAR NICOLAS FRESEDO
and ASTOR PIAZZOLLA

LAS FURIAS

By ASTOR PIAZZOLLA

LLUEVE SOBRE BROADWAY

By RAOUL COHZALES
and ASTOR PIAZZOLLA

LOS POSEIDOS

By YVES PAUL MARTIAL PUECH
and ASTOR PIAZZOLLA

MADE IN USA

By ASTOR PIAZZOLLA

MI EXALTACION

By ASTOR PIAZZOLLA

MISTERIOSA VIDA

By GUY FAVREAU
and ASTOR PIAZZOLLA

NUEVO MUNDO

By ASTOR PIAZZOLLA

PRESENTANIA

By ROBERT AUGUSTE ENGEL
and ASTOR PIAZZOLLA

D.S. al Fine

PSICOSIS

By ASTOR PIAZZOLLA

RECUERDO NEW YORK

By ASTOR PIAZZOLLA

1.

To next section

2.

Fine

2nd time D.C. al Fine
(Key change is for D.C. only)

REVIRADO

By ASTOR PIAZZOLLA

ROMANTICO IDILIO
(Sans ta présence)

By GUY FAVREAU, ALBERT ABRAHAM,
BEN SOUSSAN and ASTOR PIAZZOLLA

SE TERMINO
(C'est fini)

By ASTOR PIAZZOLLA

SUAVIDAD

By ASTOR PIAZZOLLA

TANGO CHOC
(Doudou)

By ASTOR PIAZZOLLA

TANGUISIMO

By ASTOR PIAZZOLLA

D.C. al Fine

TE QUIERO TANGO

By ASTOR PIAZZOLLA

TODO FUÉ

By DIANA PIAZZOLLA
and ASTOR PIAZZOLLA

YO CANTO UN TANGO

By ASTOR PIAZZOLLA

About Astor Piazzolla

Astor Piazzolla (1921–1992) was the foremost composer and ambassador of tango music, who carried the signature sound of Argentina to clubs and concert halls around the world.

Piazzolla was born in 1921 in Mar del Plata, on the coast south of Buenos Aires, but lived in New York City from 1924 to 1937. In New York the young Piazzolla tuned into the vibrant jazz scene and bandleaders such as Duke Ellington and Cab Calloway. At age 12, he received his first bandoneon, a type of button accordion that is the principal voice of tango, and began playing music from the classical repertoire. Soon after his family returned to Argentina in 1937, Piazzolla joined the popular tango orchestra of Aníbal Troilo and—while still a teenager—established himself as a talented bandoneon player and arranger.

In Argentina, Piazzolla continued to study classical music, too, with the composer Alberto Ginastera and others. In 1954, Piazzolla's composition "Buenos Aires" won him a scholarship to study in Paris with Nadia Boulanger, who encouraged him to find his own voice by tapping into his passion for tango. Back in Argentina in the late 1950s, Piazzolla did just that, laying the groundwork for what become known as *tango nuevo*—new tango.

In 1960 he formed his seminal group Quinteto Tango Nuevo, featuring bandoneon alongside violin, guitar, piano, and bass. In the ensuing years Piazzolla's music increasingly used dissonance, metrical shifts, counterpoint, and other techniques inspired by modern classical composition and jazz orchestras. In Argentina, where tango is a source of national pride and identity, some tango purists were incensed by these radical departures from tradition, and in the late 1960s even Argentina's military government criticized Piazzolla for being too avant-garde.

Piazzolla left behind a huge body of music—more than 750 works—and classic recordings such as *Adiós Nonino* and *Tango: Zero Hour*, as well as collaborations with artists as diverse as poet/author Jorge Luis Borges (*El Tango*), jazz vibraphonist Gary Burton (*The New Tango*), and the Kronos Quartet (*Five Tango Sensations*). In 1986, Piazzolla's music was featured in the Broadway hit *Tango Argentino*. In 2001 Amadeus Press published *Astor Piazzolla: A Memoir*, the remarkable life story (as told to journalist Natalio Gorin) of one of the 20th century's true musical iconoclasts.